PROPS

"Coval echoes Allen Ginsberg in his spiritual revolt, cosmic vision, and longing for multicultural transcendence. In boldly beautiful and outspoken hip-hop manifestos...and a Studs Terkelesque openness to humankind's countless stories, fuel Coval's percussive calls for compassion and connection."

– DONNA SEAMAN   AMERICAN LIBRARY ASSOCIATION, BOOKLIST

"Voice of the new Chicago...brilliant, funny, magnificent, and intensely personal...should stand up there with the work of Carl Sandburg, and I don't say that lightly."

– RICK KOGAN   CHICAGO TRIBUNE

"Chicago has an identity so strong it makes other cities look ambivalent by comparison. It's not the prettiest city, but it has nothing to hide...everyone here is nose-to-the-grindstone, even the writers...like Kevin Coval, the city's unofficial poet laureate."

– ADAM MANSBACH   THE BOSTON GLOBE

"Coval's greatest strength is his rhythmic, beautiful prose...he's relatable — and likeable — for his remarkable honesty and boyish romanticism, his studied understanding of race and class, his unflinching faith in hip-hop culture and his willingness to speak truth to power, no matter what the personal cost."

– STACEY DUGAN   URB

"There is nothing 'everyday' about the brash, unbridled wail of Kevin Coval. A spirited spitter of pinpoint and necessary stanzas, Kevin displays a stunning knowledge of the human heartbeat as well as the frailties and strengths of those of us tied to its drum. Blessed with a signature voice is that shaman/lyricist/rebel/teacher, KC is at the forefront of a new aesthetic and *Everyday People* is the revolutionary rulebook that has come to guide us, none too gently, into an era that will change everything."

– PATRICIA SMITH   AUTHOR OF *TEAHOUSE OF THE ALMIGHTY*

"In the tradition of Gwendolyn Brooks, Kevin Coval is fierce enough to excavate the beauty and horror of our time, offering us bold and centered meditations, reporting what Chicago looks like in the hip hop era. *Everyday People* points us past our fears to possibilities."

– BAKARI KITWANA   AUTHOR OF *THE HIP HOP GENERATION*

Cover art & book design by Brett Neiman
Sampled map used in cover art by permission of Jane Addams Hull House Museum.

ISBN: 978-0-9708012-7-2

Printed in the United States of America by Total Printing Systems for EM Press, L.L.C.

Second Printing, 2008

EM PRESS
24041 S. Navajo Dr.
Channahon, IL 60410
WWW.EM-PRESS.COM

EVERYDAY PEOPLE

poems by KEVIN COVAL

TABLE OF CONTENTS

**PARTING THE RED, WHITE, AND BLUES
(A HIP-HOP POETICA)**

UP.S. (UTOPIAN POST-SCRIPT)

INTRODUCTION

We have a poet here, speaking eloquently and urgently in the languages of the missing. Chicago is his map and is peopled by the poet's people: the left out, the lonely, women of beauty and quiet, men dodging in and out of sunlight, often underground feeding an economy that only needs or wants them for their underpaid labor and closed-mouthness.

Kevin Coval's Chicago is a cultural quilt. He has indeed walked the city. From barbershops in Buck Town to corner stores, cafes, and musical hotspots on the south, west, and north sides, "under the common wealth of forced gas heat, open kitchen / ovens and corrupt politicians. this city and country are the same / beauty, at first glance." A kind of burning pot where the wretched underfed converges to "work in the dirt of empire." He is a poet who seldom underestimates the danger and magnetism of the city. His work is political but caring, accurate and defining — poetry that cries meaning to be used as a weapon and self-development forcing frequent smiles of agreement.

Everyday People reveals the poet's eye watching the people who make cities work; the same people who occupy the literature of Howard Zinn, Lerone Bennett Jr., Adrienne Rich, Robert Bly, Studs Terkel, Amiri Baraka, and Gwendolyn Brooks.

Clearly Coval is a wanderer, like Wendell Berry, and has staked out his territory, the cityscapes — densely populated, multi-cultural and, often, dangerous. He is a hip-hop poet who reads — not exactly an oxymoron. This book is a tribute to the shoulders of past artists he stands upon: musicians and activists such as Jane Addams, Neruda, Baldwin, Marquez, Houston, Wu-Tang Clan, Abraham Joshua Heschel, and a host of others...with Nelson Algren hovering above the lot.

U.S. Poet Laureate Charles Simic writes, "To see language for what it is one needs the line, and later the larger field of the stanza, and so on." Coval's lines slap us with his ideas, word music as revelation, connected always to teaching and learning.

Coval's writing is close to perfection in the last section: Parting the Red, White, and Blues (A Hip-Hop Poetica). These poems are hopeful, poetically optimistic, with words that fight — words in a clean and current distilling of where we are in this country.

Kevin Coval questions white presumptions and more. In the poem "white," a post 9/11 narrative, Coval offers:

> "white is american as nativity lambs and puppet governments, pawn brokers shuffling hot bodied oddities in the trunk of memory. american as blue blood anglo-phile incest chlorine gene pools, white as Sally Hemmings children, white as Israel's government wasp swarms and perpetual stingers. white is the color of oil company presidents who send non-white kids to war. white is american as forged epistemologies and counterfeit eponyms..."

Kevin Coval, like contemporary Chicago jazz vocalist Kurt Elling, "is the white guy praying in black tongues." And as he continues his search for Nelson Algren and his own heart, he captures the minds and imaginations of readers ready for a change and challenge. Coval makes a definitive transition from slinging shots to healing, understanding and writing poetry that embodies a historical sensibility that in the final analysis can make a difference.

DR. HAKI R. MADHUBUTI

Poet,
University Distinguished Professor,
Professor of English and Director of the Master of Fine Arts in Creative Writing at Chicago State University
Founder and Publisher of Third World Press

for eboo patel,
whose hands(&heart) are big
enough to hold our city/country
in its *confluence of contradictions*.

*HE IS SPEAKING TO HER. THE ONLY SOUND IN THE WHOLE CITY
IS HIS HEART BEGGING HER LIGHT, TO COME CLOSER.*

– TONY FITZPATRICK CHICAGO SKY #4

he said, i write what i see / write to make it right / don't like where i be

– LUPE FIASCO HIP-HOP SAVED MY LIFE

EVERYDAY PEOPLE

SUNRISE

it is 6:13 a.m.

on the phone
her voice, a hushed arousal.

from the bed, looking east
the skyline, a silhouette.
hancock erect.

the sun
birthing out of Lake Michigan's wet mouth
blushes Chicago a rainbow;

brick roofed zenith,
the peeled skin of orange,
honey like the roads
promised, the shallow pockets
chasing them, all the blues, melancholic to indigo, follow Black,
crowning the body of lakeshore:

awake are the alleys scribbled with tribal pictures.
awake are the newspaper trucks hauling dead trees.
awake are the waitresses flipping on pots of coffee.
awake are the migrants hoping in the cold.

awake are the mothers still waiting on their sons.
awake are the corner store clerks opening iron gates.
awake are the teachers lesson planning long commutes.
awake are the pigeons circling lonely rooftops.

awake are the factories breathing grey smoke.

awake are the cabbies going home to raise their family.
awake are the stray dogs packed in Humboldt Park.

awake are the L trains thundering thru the sky.
awake are the buses rumbling thru the streets.

awake are the fallen risen from Lower Wacker.
awake are the fishermen older than the water.

awake are the children putting on their uniforms.
awake are the workers who will greet this sun.

awake is the sky holding all the city.
awake is the sky holding all the city.

awake is the sky

awake is the sky
awake is the sky
awake is the sky

awake is the sky
awake is the sky
awake is the sky
awake is the sky

THE CORNER STORE

at Wood and Division
sells beef jerky and sandalwood incense,
clorox bleach and brass monkey, Mexican and Polish baked
goods for those forced to flee the neighborhood.

in the summer i get gatorade here
after playing ball in the schoolyard
at Anderson Elementary where my Zadie,
George Coval, walked from his apartment
at 1750 W. Haddon. nothing but a giant marble
flick from the two bedroom he shared with half
a boat-load of Russian cousins
forced to flee cossacks.

                        in Yemen
it is summer all the time,
or so says the owner, his mouth raised
toward the falling white, hair on his lip, talking
through wisps of incense rising in front
of the counter, on the first snow this winter
where in the window behind him, old style neon
beckons a six pack, and behind this sign
grey sags over the city like a beer
gut about to burst.

the first snow, a blanket
before the city sloshes
its boots and tires through
fallen frozen clouds.

                                        it's summer there,
but everyone wants to be here,
he says.

                                        he means america
at the same time he means Chicago,
the immense burden of cold and wind
his dream, still dreamt. at times
toward realized, this america,
this Chicago, this why the world works
under the common wealth of forced gas heat,
open kitchen ovens and corrupt politicians.
this city/country are the same
beauty at first glance
and after toiling in the rush-hour commute
grit sticks and melts the bones
of those called to work in the dirt of empire
of country with its *wretched refuse*
of city proud to be alive, its *lifted head singing*,
gigantic, impossible demands:
to dream the dream, like a still
landscape of all
that is possible.

REASONS TO BE LATE TO A FAMILY DINNER

the merengue of pigeons, swirling
from the spires of the Yolocalli Youth Museum
over the Rudy Lozano Public Library at 18th St.
and Blue Island; perching, waiting, resuming
the same pattern in the pilgrimage to welcome day.

city workers who blast intimacies over jackhammers
loud enough for the whole neighborhood to hear.

the monk on the bus, heavily robed,
though the sun is out, snores
like the engine, drowning silence to sleep.

at Dominick's, two men
in the deli section laugh
the joke like kolache
on their tongues.

stand in front of the citrus section for hours,
                like in Amsterdam
                        the first time
                                mushrooms, dazed
        skins   ablaze,
                        the clerk said
                                        leave!

        but offered an orange and grapefruit.

at the cash register
a woman
who rushes bar codes thru red scanners eight hours a day
is smiling,

will that be credit or debit, hun?
delight in the assonance, the hard,
short *e's*, the final drawn hum of *hun*.

ride the back of the bus home
to she
who waits in the bedroom
gathering enough information to make
the border patrol almost forget
her passport is foreign.

when she exhales, shoulders curl toward her chin,
hands fold to her chest, shrouded in a shawl to keep
cold out or pray in a temple of cotton sheets.

she will ask to take a nap. (say *yes*)

watch her body rise with air
like a balloon tied to her son's hand
on a summer day near the Des Plaines River.

fingers sneak behind her ear like a whisper,
wisps of hair line her spine. measure her
curves like a surveyor; pear-shaped shoulders,
the angularity of elbows, the gentle roundness of bottom,
her body a museum of irreverent geometry.

LATE TO YOU ON THE BLUE LINE

i am
on the blue line
late to you,
on the blue line
coming late
to you, but
i am
coming. on mass
transit underground
underarm malodorous
hot bowel basement station
i am
coming in a car
with no air, hands held
to heaven, silver
sticks hold me steady
packed secretaries
at my elbows listen to moans
of loneliness in their head
phones
i am
coming to you
late, but
i am coming.
hoping you will still
still at the window sill
cotton dress and pretty
and maybe you will
and maybe you will
not, but i am coming
still, on the blue line.
i am

on the blue line
that screams in the sky
over Milwaukee Ave
over lots of empty lots
where green grass weeds
where we sometimes walk
near Puerto Rico's children
who blue blood lines
red line away, who blue
badges make bleed
sometimes
i am
empty handed
cuz the corner store
closed, i am coming
late to you
still
on the blue line
that threads the eyes
of loop, sews a split
smile over the city
i am
on the blue line
frozen still
between Jackson
and Washington, still
late to you
i am
coming on the blue line
(and sometimes i pray
it's never too) late
to come to you.

WET JULY

we need the windows
open, fans turned high,
the sauna of air's mouth,
wet.   july.
we came
after walking
on Roscoe
past the coach
house i was born in,
after Melrose Diner
and Reckless Records,
after the 1:20 p.m. start
on a tuesday, the only
afternoon this month
we can give ourselves
and schedules fully to
the other.
we pull
and unfasten
and lick
and wet
july is a towel
wrung on a mattress
in Wrigleyville, 2 blocks
from the field 40,000 dream
81 times a year in ivy green
straight backed, hard
plastic seats, holding more
cupped hands in prayer
than a church.

your bedroom
window is open,
fans turned high
their screams
exclamate
my name
in your
mouth,
hot,
wet,
july.

MISS CHICAGO

Like loving a woman with a broken nose, you may well find
lovelier lovelies. But never a lovely so real.

– NELSON ALGREN

of course she's a waitress.
she drinks more than you.
jameson shots and budweiser
or old style if it's a bar-b-q
in summer. she'll eat cheeseburgers
rare or hockey puck,
no qualms or self-consciousness,
sit on your lap, mouth full of meat,
stick her tongue in your throat.

she is beautiful. a fine ass woman
no other man would argue, but
she does wear braces or doesn't
wear a bra or has cracked lips,
a crooked nose, big ears, inappropriate
tattoos, a series of boyfriends who beat her.

she wears one piece cotton dresses
and paints her toenails Black. she smokes
and swears and dropped outta college. she
lived in Milwaukee and is from Dubuque
or Harvey or off some Polack boat or Puerto Rico
or Bridgeport for christ's sake. she's no jew.
she's a catholic and could give a fuck.

she has cold sores and possibly more.
she took you home the first night you met
at the bar she works at, but didn't sleep
with you. that was the second date, a week

later, after you took her out to dinner, fought
over the bill, demanded she leave
the tip in cash cuz she knows how it is
to hide.

she loves walking near train yards;
metra and amtraks on Roosevelt,
the abandoned bridge on North Ave.,
freight yards west on Cermak, she'll
point out morning doves, tails flapping
on a telephone line, a barren tree on a street
filled with bloom, every flower raised and wild
she knows to call them by their names she
learned with her Gram in a garden in Pilsen
or Omaha.

she knows the perfect date is a monday afternoon.
she's hung over. the sun is out. you are on the patio
at Irazu, a Costa Rican sandwich and burrito shop
she's never been to, but it could be any ethnic shack
with outdoor seats, crank umbrellas and something
cold to drink. she's gotta be to work at 6, a massage
client before that, or other side hustles, so after lunch
you drink tap water from a pitcher in the fridge.
she undresses in the sticky sweat box that is your third
floor greystone rental apartment and it's a good thing
your roommate isn't home cuz she's loud with your name
in her mouth. her hair a stringy wet mop, your bed filled
with water and all that sweat. she will rinse off
in the shower and dry herself in front of the window fan.
she will leave in a car with Iowa plates, unregistered in the city
still, after seven years. before she leaves she will
kiss you long and hard on your mouth and you will
not want her to leave, but she's gotta be to work
which means she's always going to be   leaving.

LEAVING NORMAL

at the bimonthly poetry slam in Normal, Illinois
i wanted a beverage with bubbles to settle my belly.
then i wanted ice cream cuz the sign said it was homemade
and the girl behind the counter said she can make me
a root beer float and was thick and beautiful and reminded me
of Anna, a pretty, half Philippina-half Ukrainian mid-west suburban girl
whose parents met at a hospital.
                                        but i am in Normal,
IL.
the float is delicious. the reading
feels like a variety show in the death
of summer camp. except for Robbie Q,
the host. this is his last night in Normal.
he is moving to Chicago where he is known
for a poem about muppets. he is in the middle
of his goodbye which is a monologue about all
the people at the reading. he is giving their stories
back to them, and the people are delighted
to see a local boy, from some other somewhere
no one has ever heard of, leave or move on or search
for bigger audiences who might not smile as much
or appreciate his plaid sport coat, who might
forget his face, his name a coaster in a corner bar
where hopefully he could talk to someone.

                          tonight is Robbie Q
in top form, a big fish
hoping to fry beneath the sizzle
of second city spotlights. he is
emptying five years from his pockets;
stones, string, change he's collected.
the people standing now, Robbie has gone

quiet before their applause. faces he stretched into laughter
and sung into mist, he can pick out of a crowd and paint names on
faces who dream his dream, like a heaven (or city) that awaits.

SLEEPING WITH A STRANGER

breathing in unison
our bodies held the bottom
crook of z. a foot apart,
symmetrical spoons
mirroring each other's curves
on a train from New York.

my seatmate
68 years old,
a retired postal worker
living in Jamaica, Queens,
born among fishermen
in South Carolina,
looked like what a skinny boy
with ashy knees grows up to be.

the smallest kid on the playground
who put the most sugar in the lemonade
and loves his mama like he loved his wife
since 1947 when he got back from Germany

welcomed home by Jim Crow
and segregated lunch counters
and no jobs and no GI Bill
and no more family south

he traveled north
like blues to big apples
poisoned by industrialist whispers
Johnny Appleseed wormed in the backroom
of former Cotton Clubs turned mills.
befriended poets, musicians

turned machinists in Harlem,
canners and dockworkers later
junkies home from Asia
with demons in their veins.

the first of a four-day train ride
to see his daughter and grandchildren
in Los Angeles.

he had six tapes:
three Muddy Waters
two Etta James
one Sarah Vaughn
a can of peanuts
an army green derby
shielded eyes from light

hands shone like wet mud
bones like granite beneath jeans
sharp into my thigh as he moved
in the too few hours of sleep

chest rising beneath wisps of breathing,
heart pumping sweet whistles thru Ohio

as he turned in night
i followed his lead
around the dance floor
of two coach seats.

MESSING: (A)ROUND

will we will we ever settle down, down, forever sketching clouds
now, we crowd the towns around now and whisper to the clouds, how

will we will we ever ever settle? we wishing wishing wishing
upon a cloud, a day, a dreams all day, want to play play, no career my fear or 401k

k? is how you spell my name name, get my 1040 right, death and thumb tacks
hold heros on my office wall, my office y'all, no office at all, a closet in the back

apartment i rent, rent each month write a check, 1st of the month check, check, health care
money spent, out of pocket, every check, every month a sport i report like Chet Choppock,

got it? will we will we stop sketching clouds? hold hope upside down? public speaking
loud, rush like division streets crowds, inertia moving, never never settle, apartments

apartments, books in cardboard boxes, cds in case logics, hip-hop to heavy metal, settle
settle sediment, shhhhhhh...gentle men, settle in quiet like dust in the bottom of the river,

she wrote her number in my hand with mud, now i call her river. ten numbers in my hand
and ten numbers right behind her. i'ma find her, among the crowds of towns, travel around,

public speaking loud. where you at, where you from, hold my hope inside your eyes now,
your eyes now, fold inside my eyes now, i want to see you see you, be seen besides the scene,

i mean will we will we live among the forests of steel and rusted beams, mid-west be the best
flat fields of soy beans, miles ya boy dreams, sketch Chicago lovely, lovely the city beautiful

brutal ugly, beautiful brutal youthful dis-a-hipster smugly, ugly yuppies trust fund lucky,
Daley must be holding a bottle of bleach upside down, turning the blues to white, beautiful

brutal ugly! forefather dollars, condo model scholars, hollerin holler, beautiful brutal ugly!
she beautiful brutal ugly! sketch Chi-city lovely, when will she love me? holler when she love me,

holy unfolding, she beautiful brutal ugly! i'll holler when she love me! holler when she hold me!
holler cuz she know me! holler because she holy! sketch Chi-city holy! she beautiful brutal lovely!

ALL FALL DOWN

mourning
won't take long.
there is a week
the trees will be
on fire. a day
later leaves
the sidewalk
a mattress of autumn.
yellow on the ground
forgives the sun
for not coming out
in ten days. Kanye's
mother passed. his words
anthems to rise to
on the solitary walk
to the train. the world
quiets and colds
and you are not here
anymore. you left
or were pushed away
like all the workers
the city promised
to hold forever
and raise their children
in public schools.
the first snow falls
the night before thanksgiving.
i return from a meal
you didn't attend,
wrap myself in an afghan
your mother weaved

CHICKEN A LA TONY THE TIGER

we'd sit at the kitchen table for four
in a triangle.   Eric to her right,
me on the left, mom's back to the stove
and counter top, eyes facing the wallpaper
where she hung wicker fans or the mini tv,
thursday nights when she let us watch
the cosby show.

if we complained of a bbq repeat
no spoon or back of the hand, but silence
as if she didn't hear.

the night my father went bankrupt
he brought 2 huge bags to my mom's house: one clear
sack filled with seventy pounds of frozen chicken breasts
and a Black garbage bag, the kind you collect fall in,
stuffed with a seemingly endless supply of frosted flakes.

the frosted flakes lived on top of the refrigerator.
every morning, for over a year, we'd scoop a bowl
out its limp body, slurp our inheritance
before school, trying to drown out its plastic
predictable sweetness in skim milk.

mom made a cookbook that year,
hundreds of ways to change chicken breasts:
diced and seasoned, creamy cold, chopped,
sautéed, broiled, soaked, minced, sliced
potatoes, peas, corn on the side, cheese
on top, shredded in pasta, rice, cous cous
dipped in wine, butter, oil, honey, anything
for a slight shift in flavor.

but it was the night she rolled the chicken
in frosted flakes, centered them on the table
like she was the sitcom's straight man,
that our laughter bust like stitches, tears
flooding, a broken dam.

WHAT IT'S LIKE TO DELIVER PIZZAS IN YOUR 50S
after Patricia Smith

your ex-wife tells your kids
she saw it coming. your friends
offer to write you a check and won't
return your phone calls. whispers float
from women, who peck their husbands
to cancer, over your premature grave
like Kaddish. your family brings full plates
of Sabbath leftovers. you are working
without a day of rest and they won't
return your phone calls. bosses twenty
years your junior treat you like you are
diseased, lazy, a schmuck down on his
luck, a horse calling for the shotgun.

it's blistered finger tips, lost addresses, gas station
pee breaks, side streets with tree names, doorbells
14 year old princes answer and never tip. $5/hr
plus a buck a pie. your '84 astro van curling 200,
000 miles. aramis in the glove box, pine fresh
around the rear view, John Denver in the cassette deck,
a picture of me and E and you, tucked in the sun block
above your head.

it's rushing and receipts, hot cheese in your lap,
men your age glimpse what they fear or
disgust. it's an alley with a gun in your face
the spasms shooting through your body
as you drive away.

REALITY

in the middle of the blacktop playground,
the worst emcee battle i've ever seen.

judges is blunted and salty
been in the sun and Chicago's underground
too long. no love or recognition / no ROC chain
only open mic cannibal nights ripping each other
new orifices to complain from.

the crowd was all hype
ready to rock steady
but hip-hop was mad late.
2 p.m. meant 5:30. emcees were tired
stuttering pre-written rhymes with less punch
lines than prom nights during prohibition.
i mean the shit was so wack
jermaine dupri woulda liked it

D- couplets from B+ of the Spastic Bunch
      true-man i drop bombs, like Nas- half man half amazing
      your moms rides my knob like affirmative action for caucasians

the lone female of the Get Rich Quick Collective
      punk emcees is stupid, on my menstrual cycle u couldn't flow fam
      protect yrself i spit soldiers, a wooden horse poking holes in your tro-jan

Comma Kazi of the GnV crew, gangsta n vegan
      esoteric hilarity you couldn't shine on polaris beams paris dreams of Josephine
      Baker shakin her can-can, autistic mystic i'm Dustin Hoffman in Rain Man

and it don't stop
or didn't for what seemed like 100 rounds

i wished had been Russian
roulette

cept there's one kid in the park
cept i hadn't seen him for a minute
heard he got knocked,
cept he's here now
cept his face is all fucked up
like it caught a bullet

Reality used to spit on Damen Ave
when Wicker Park was Latino
families and gentrification loomed
larger than white folks weaving yarn
in a snow storm.

Reality played the back
wall posted like no bills
the whole afternoon just chillin
minutes into the intro of dusk
as the sky over Chi dawned a Black cape.

after the all the spit and metaphorical blood
spilled, everybody's mama dragged here
with out their consent, two thousand n-words
piled in the corner next to gun-pen analogies,
reputations shot to pieces

Reality listened to the weak
end. walked into the middle
of the ring, took a deep breath
and exhaled a torrent, a giant
cloud emptying its belly.

Reality washed the whole city
or at least the park or at least

the blacktop or at least the wind
that moment, his song blast
slapping ear drums
like skin pulled taut,
caught in the face
of a bullet.

THE DTC CREW PAYS TRIBUTE TO DICE

they are an odd couple.
Abbott and Costello after crack,
hip-hop renaissance men.

Jon writes rhymes, graffiti, plays congas, fixes cars and sound systems,
studies conspiracy theories, medicinal marijuana laws, caporiea and breaking.
his legs and long torso wind scissor in the helicopter, arms sculpted in stone.

Pele writes graffiti, beat boxes in the cipher, but he is a b-boy in the tradition.
boogaloo on grey stoops. he'd drop to the concrete to show you his latest flair
and footwork. his body, a metal instrument he polishes on the varnish of empty
gymnasiums.

best friends
since the block was safe to play on
when the street lights glowed yellow
and their mothers called them home for supper.
Jon's mom served fish sticks most nights,
Pele's arroz con dules,
so Jon usually went home with Pele.

Jon and Pele were taking DICE,
the newest member of the **DTC** crew,
bombing

DTC
Destroy **T**he **C**ity
Don't **T**rust **C**ops
Diss **T**oys **C**onstantly

bars were way past closing. only the homeless
and 24/7 convenient store clerks were awake.
them and the DTC crew bounding from rooftops,
high wire walking train lines, pausing on the apex

of a parking garage to listen to the galaxy, a silent
arcade where only the stars would shoot.

the police were also awake though
and the police don't like art or kids
of color. the police chased the DTC crew
along the sky decks of unfinished condos
under the dome of night, moon spotlight.
cops and muralists, armed with guns and spray cans,
respectively, criss-crossing L tracks and apartments
like cat and mice, colonizer and colonized.

DICE

fell   thru an opening
of roof; a loft in rehab, remade pretty for someone
who don't live there

                                                        yet.

after the funeral Jon and Pele said they were out,
two best friends drunk on homage, throwing up
a thousand whispers on concrete so the angels would know
for sure who to take.

a forty-eight hour bombing spree. every stop sign,
mailbox, newspaper machine, base of light post, alley
dumpster, crane, city vehicle, abandoned store front
scribbled DICE in fresh white and silver tipped handstyles.

and to the west
on a slanted silver storage roof, eight stories
above the interstate, half a city block long,
an orange, red, and yellow burner ran the sky like sunset

DICE (RIP)
burned in the western sky
weeks before graffiti blasters noticed.

waiting on the bus
we looked and wondered
a secret moment to ourselves
who is DICE? how do i mourn?

ODE TO THE OPEN MIC HOST

for Robert in Bellingham and all those who practice democracy

how many hats do you wear
flyers you print, emails you send,
money you shoestring out your pocket
to stick forty bucks into the hand of your feature,
give twenty to the sound guy and tip the waitress
half the night's tab. to secure a venue
means you'll tell Christine, who owns the coffee shop,
you'll be back in two weeks.

you listen,
like a therapist, to the desires
and dissatisfactions of retail salesmen,
administrative assistants, school teachers,
and college kids broke on daddy's allowance.

how many rants,
identity affirmations,
workshop experiments,
which neither work
nor are experimental,
slumming professors,
low-minded high journal
note taking one-time
no-show idiots who think
they should be famous,
have you sat thru.

all these guys
part-time comedians,
jokes you've heard
every other week
for five years.

how many
old white dudes
in pleated khakis
and collarless denim
shirts buttoned to the top
have read twelve sheets
of AB AB dragon poems
and left the mic feeling you
not only were not rude
but kind of enjoyed their work
and when you mentioned
there is a three minute limit
thought this was a general
announcement not a condemnation.

you must get sick of all the voices.
the end of every sentence twisted
into a question, the homophobic
failed emcees who do this poetry shit
cuz the industry just ain't ready dog,
the hippie mystic Mayan calendar goddess
chanting ohm breaths thru nose rings,
white girl blues singers, angry white boys,
Asian-Black nationalists, how many
hallmark cards about losing a grandparent
could the world of your psyche withstand.

there isn't even a stage,
as much as a space you carved, a mic
needed only to amplify the nervous
and virgins, the soft spoken and humble.
the bellowers among us can hit the back
window that separates the cappuccino machines
hot breath from main street strollers
or latter rush hour store clerks going home,
                                        finally.

unbelievably, you don't really play favorites.
the handful of half-decent writers, all of whom
you drink with before and after the show, you call to
orate with the same enthusiasm and kindness, the same
general interest and discernment as you do all
on your list. you tribute our stories, our names
emblazoned for a moment of night, fleeting
on the flashing billboard of your tongue.

WHAT TONY TELLS ME AFTER A READING IN SOUTHERN ILLINOIS

Tony is a union man.
taper and paint mixer,
makes good money, to spend
on NASCAR and big screens.

Tony lives in O'Fallon.
drives to Edwardsville to drink.
tonight he's helping a buddy
move after divorce.

most his buddies are firemen.
they grew up playing together:
firemen, cops, cowboys, ghosts
in the graveyard til supper served.

Tony's hands are like blocks
of meat the butcher would donate
to the alley. Tony has a goatee
looks like a heavy Dan Quisenberry

or Goose Gossage, relief pitchers
in the '80s. relief pitchers are firemen
called to extinguish the away teams'
comeback in the top of the ninth inning.

Tony talked about the firemen he knew,
how when Black families moved to town
Tony's friends protected the other homes
with a white moat of flame resistant foam.

they'd make sure it'd look like arson
or an insurance scam or electric mishap
or not, cuz the police play on the same team
in a softball league. after the game they drink

uniformed men trained to hang
bottles of jim beam upside down.

GLOBALIZATION:
THE LAST FACTORY TOWN IN AMERICA OR WHAT I LEARNED WHILE PLAYING PEORIA

1

Peoria, Il is the home of Richard Pryor. that's all i knew
before reading at the bradley student center. the king lived there
which meant Black people lived there, worked hard to raise their family.

2

hotel pére marquette was built in 1927.
its list of celebrity guests begins with liberace
includes dan quayle and Andre the Giant.

i was given two large gold keys with jagged teeth.
room 938. pressed 9 in the elevator. the 10 above
read CATERPILLAR, then skipped to 11.

3

caterpillar makes me think of green and yellow
which are john deere colors. caterpillar's colors are
Black and yellow like the Latin Kings.

4

Brian McKinney, a red-haired senior, looks 15.
wears a kelly green shirt when he picks me up in a car
his parents bought the summer he spent in Ireland.

he is an electrical engineering student
says caterpillar throws millions at his department
to entice graduates to stay, to design, to sell more machinery.

5

Katrina, less a hurricane, more a summer rain, wants to teach social studies.
schools are bifurcated along class lines, she says. one for caterpillar executives'
and bradley professor kids. one for the children of janitors.

6

we are in The World Café. i am eating a cajun tofu wrap.
they tell me which clubs play hip-hop,
what their parents do, what they study, what they dream.

they remember a protest
at caterpillar. something about bulldozers
used in israel.

7

there is only one plant left. Peoria used to be a factory town.
america out sources Brown and Yellow hands to assemble
all the products we buy and ship in hulls overseas.

8

song of globalization

it hits me
like a ton of bricks
collapsed on the living
rooms of doctors.

Black and gold
lettering. the king
corporation. military
free base   ....

Richard running down
the street on fire.

Peoria. king
of tractors, wheels,
metal cranes plowing
front doors of kitchens
grandmas roll pita in,

a buried memory. debris,
Rachel Corrie. a fiction
AmericaIsrael says is
fiction. a foxhole
for terrorist sympathies,
which is to say families,
men who no longer hear
rain on tin rooftops,
pins drizzled in rapid fire.

Richard running down the street
on fire
                    rockets,
plastic bullets
hollow tips.
borderless
corporate,
AmericaIsrael
supporters.
education departments
keep columbus heroic,
the aggressor patriotic,
the militarized, self-defensive,
the resistant, a ghost
traitor, rubble under
the table, a field
of gravestones, an assembly
line of sweet voices who will never
speak of what was here
prior to before.

PASSING GENERATIONS

Rose tells the room her granmother was a Black woman
though she is paler than the dying
                              tips of white petals

she says her granmother was a Black woman
raped by a white man
                       when such occurrences went unsaid
a common practice
                   like pumping water from a well

Rose says her granmother was Black
but her baby was so light she could be served on Main St.
in the penny candy store   in Evansville, IN   in 1962
and bring change home to her Black mother   on the side of town
where garbage wasn't picked up and factory boys went   after drunk
                       & 3rd shift

Rose's mother,
a school girl who never brought friends home,
who slipped through hallways her whole life
without a co-worker or classmate ever calling bluff,
bore children white like she
                     & her husband
Rose's father
                     who all-white unioned
                     blue collar lost job,
                     blamed immigrants
                     & Jesse Jackson.

Rose tells the room
                     a quiet gathering of university secretaries and a handful of
                     Black undergrads who've organized the lunch & learn panel
                     discussion at Vincennes University   Vincennes, IN

her husband is Black,
they have two kids

                        the boy looks like his father, hair a juniper shrub she says, is six.
                        the girl looks like Rose, skin a lampshade, pellucid, yellow, nine.

Rose's mother   whose mother was a Black woman
coddles the girl, makes dresses for her dolls, teaches her card games, cookie making
                    but
Rose tells the room
                    her mother,
whose mother was a Black woman,
won't let her Black granchild sleep
in her house, won't take him
out for a drive or a visit
to the cemetery where the Black
mother, granmother, great-granmother
is buried
on the other side of town
where garbage still don't get picked up
and histories lie in the skin
of children
                 waiting
                 for their mothers
& fathers
to claim them.

THE SON OF EVERY WOMAN

in Bennington, VT, i pulled into a gas station
off Rt. 7, after looking fruitlessly at the rent-a-car road
atlas for directions. a woman in an old butter Cadillac
introduced me to her fat beagle named Molly in the backseat.
Molly got out of the car and the woman pulled a napkin
from her purse and fed Molly what must have been
a quarter pound of roast beef. Molly was huge.
her tiny legs unable to keep her belly from hitting the ground.
Molly and the woman could've been sisters: short, stumpy,
insouciant. she lived in North Bennington her whole life
said i have to go to Sonny's Blue Benn Diner for supper.
her gold earrings deflected sun. her green purple blue blazer,
quilt work. she pointed to the bend in the road i should stay
right on. her hand extended to shake mine. she held it
in her palm, perhaps to read it. said i looked like her son.

every summer since my grandfather passed
and my grandmother remarried and relocated
to Newton, MA, i've made a trip in july to see her.
i take the Amtrak east for time to write, read and witness
the backyards where america stores its garbage, near automobile
cemeteries, clothes lines that air dry bed sheets, lawns that house
a series of repair projects trailed off in mid-sentence...
once in Boston, i take a green line metro train to a station
near my grandmother's apartment building. her and the husband
will be waiting when i arrive. i have a back pack, a duffle bag,
enough of a beard to tug on, a 1937 re-issued Chicago Cubs fitted cap
over my head, shaved close enough for the northeast's wet heat. a woman,
her arms a bundle of grocery bags, refuses help on the green line, asks me
to remove my hat. her stare lasts a full minute while the world takes a nap,
her eyes glass, she says i look like her son.

i am leaving the woman i love but could never tell
because we are two good friends, catching the PATH from Jersey City
back to Union Square. we spent the afternoon talking in the garden
outside her brownstone, sitting on a bench reserved for men in fedoras
and women with head wraps, hands full of breadcrumbs. i stop in a Halal market
to buy some juice. they have apricot nectar, the kind my grandmother hid in her refrigerator
friday nights when we lit candles and everyone lived in Chicago. i have exact change. the woman
behind the counter wears a silver and Black hijab. she is smiling because i have apologized
for all my pennies. i wait until she counts them. when she is finished, her hands reach
for my face, she holds it like an offering. she says her son is bearded like me, and Muslim and
fighting in the united states marine corp. this is all she says. and by now we are breathing
and tearing and human. and i leave her store and walk to a train that will take me to Manhattan.

LURED BENEATH YOUR GOLDEN, CALLING LIGHTS

after Carl Sandburg for BI and SHL

it is impossible to know you.
impossible to gather all i can
in my arms and claim to have an idea
of your immensity.

              even when i see you
on Broadway,   in white knit Kangols
and circus hoop silver bangles, your sweet roast
almond scent. even when you pull my body flat
against yours i still feel foreign, or that you
are a foreigner or that sometimes this experiment
will not last. at some point the Nigerian doctors
picking up used straws in the Angelica film center
or the Pakistani cabbie or Chilean hot pretzel vendor
or my midwestern uncle working three jobs
for child support, will collapse in your lap
with white flag or fire.
                  i've been tempted
to rent an apartment in morning
side heights, but
              you are an impossible dream
              i scream myself awake in.
too immense,
      intense,
never mine to grasp,
a Coney Island carousel
      of images,
you whirl too fast.
you are an express train,
i never know which track you'll be on.

the Indian restaurant at 94th and Amsterdam
is slide metal gates on glass windows,
i can no longer look in and see
the table we first sat at.

the all night diner
where you ordered rice pudding,
in Union Square, is a Sports Club
for people who can afford one
you have changed,
have always been
changing.

      but
      damn! you look good
      New York.
      you court me
      again.
                (again, New York)
at 3rd and Mercer
we felt like tea, i knew you
would suggest Cafe Reggio,
though i had not been there
since '94 and couldn't remember
its location or name but felt its windows
would open to the street and perfect
after-dinner in spring. sitting
in metal-wire chairs, blackberry supreme
pot steeping on the two-top wooden table,
i knew i could love you again (though i know you are not mine alone
& Chicago will not want to hear this, but...)

your civilized all-hour tomatoes!
your fresh flower tombs littering the fronts of bodegas!
your subway lines: vast and democratic!
your bootlegs sleeping on blankets like dominos!
your two model per train car city ordinance!
all those mixed babies blurring neighborhood lines!
your gold space pharaohs slanging veg patties on 125th St.!
your corner kids up late blaring Biggie out 6th floor apartment windows!
my grandfather's anglicized name tucked in a book on Ellis Island!
your Grandmaster Flash mash-ups! your Grandwizard Theodore scratch bombs!
your Afro-Diasporic Puerto Rican borough global exports!
your shtick, New York, each one of you sounds like a jew
and even italians know how to make good bagels!
you are the ultimate reality / check! the last of bastion
of schmer and empire. the american ideal gone

                                                  mad

and perfect.

WAKING UP / IN CHICAGO

the rooster is named Jorge.
he will never be eaten.
he traveled on a bus from Mexico
with the family who lives next door.
he is named for the grandfather
too old to take the trip with them.

the dual tape deck boom box
in the corner of the studio i rent
barrio blasts Public Enemy.

steam from the shower
fogs the kitchen like Sandburg's poem,
though i am allergic to cats.
soap suds my body a costume.
i draw a rib cage.

the towels mama gave me
after papa passed are yellow.

i decide which of his shirts to wear.
both are blue, one short sleeved,
sharp cut collar, a lone pocket over the heart.
the other checkered with turmeric and sage,
no buttons at the cuffs. it is cool.

sun seeps through the windows
like music of last night's street song;
reggaeton bullets tapping the window,
Norteno y Boleros hung over late into

                    this morning
where families on stooped steps laugh,
drink café con leche, mill about after the mill
or all-night diner, rest kids in the concrete
of this neighborhood, where my family wish
i didn't live
                    and this is not
the only sentiment my family shares
with these families.

                    by now
i am late, like the train,
for a job i am trying
not to have. on 18th St., Mercedes
will not make me eggs on a croissant
with sliced poblanos and avocado.
she might wave sweeping her porch
which is now an outdoor seating area
beneath the sidewalk. i will walk past
Daniel's barbershop and not get a fade.
he will be shot in three weeks for being
young and brown and on the wrong block,
out later than he knows he should. i will
return at any hour, undeterred,
no headphones only questions:
am i the pioneer
who brings colonialism like a tail wind
sending families spinning like plastic bags
in an alley, or a working class white kid
just needing some place cheap to rent,
or the child of american dreamers
whose flight broke suburban homes,
lonely. now, returning to paint
tangled legacies with ink
on white
paper.

NELSON ALGREN SQUARE IS A TRIANGLE

six Black benches
round the square triangle
like neighborhoods. metal bar benches
like prison. each bench an enclave:
Black men in sweats, sell white socks,
white men in Bears hats reek ripe cologne,
Latinos behind frutierias and paleta freezers,
two Asian men listen to water splash in the fountain,
in the middle of the square triangle young addicts
faces pierced by office supplies, huddle under cardboard
billboards, crayola letters scribbled cryptic,
Polacks, from the elderly home off Noble, feed the pigeons
bread crumbs stashed beneath their bed since the war.

     all in the square are homeless.
     all rise in the morning to clouds.
     all dine in the shadows of empire.
     all dream in the rupture of loud.

only men in the square
older than they say.
one eye on their shopping cart
swollen with construction scraps.
one hand on a cigarette, a cane
a plastic bag. the other eye
scans the new migrants
emptying the blue line:

their stroll is a stroll. a tote bag and sun
glasses, flip phone and assured futures.
they catch cabs lined along Milwaukee,

home to a sofa and fire, home to a stereo sound,
home to a bottle of red wine, a television,
an alley view, a wife for the time of now.

the men in the square triangle will talk
all afternoon. they will wander for a hundred years.
pigeons will fly away, eyed-out pieces of bread
around their necks like life preservers.

      all in the square are homeless.
      all rise in the morning to clouds.
      all dine in the shadows of empire.
      all dream in the rupture of now.

SUNDAY IS A HOLY DAY, SUNDAY IS A WORK DAY

Sharrief is in his bear blue
usher uniform. ear muffs, parka,
extra heavy wool sweater, ski gloves
bear blue, darker than royal, a navy
maybe, all over the stadium, all over
his body.

it is sunday, Sharrief works
at soldier field where men are
revered for being monsters
of the midway.

Sharrief is sitting at a café table
at the depaul student center
in lincoln park, waiting for a student
not to log off a computer so he can read
his email. a cardboard box he carried
from work warms his elbow, houses his dinner,
a piece of pizza. he will pick off the pepperoni.

Sharrief doesn't eat pork.

Sharrief is waiting
for the sun to cover the west
side in darkness, so he can
eat his slice of pizza, on this sunday
during Ramadan, waiting
in the depaul student center
where he is not enrolled, waiting
to check his email, waiting

to sleep after a sunday on the gridiron, waiting
to break his fast, waiting

for a break
in his day, waiting
for day to break, so he can
eat,
sleep,
break,
fast.

the attentive hands
of a copper hulled man
fold in his lap like birds.
brown pants muddied yellow
shirt sleeves rolled to elbows
hair combed over with pomade
slick as his mustache.

the red box at his feet
blackened from wear.
a scrub brush, cloths
pulled taut and furious
over winged tips and
squared toes, a small
red stool for stability.

fingertips the color of coal
will soon push an apartment
open in Little Village, on the sunset
side of Cook County's incarcerated.

ADORNMENT

after Zora Neale Hurston

my dj turned twenty-one tonight.
i got him a Cubs hat, a book of writing
exercises. but he is searching the sky
for arms to hold him.

the air is a wet wool blanket
you can't wrestle your feet from.

on a park bench i unbutton my shirt
and wait for the bus.
                              it is late
June. the moon has risen orange.
the sky discolored by the veil of ghost industries,
quiet stretched across the street like a yawn.

from the north
the din of kettle drums tickle my ear.
there is a wheel chair spinning south
down Damen Ave., red and white lights, whirling
like an ambulance. the chair holds a funk band.
the chair is draped in a cape of beads that scrape
the potholed Black top. a boom box harnessed
on handles no one pushes. sound tracks grey rubber wheels,
silver spoke-d rims, the chiseled arms that move them.

his cell phone riots, high pitched
keyboard notes and thumping base bars
like Bootsy might be calling.
he wears a purple headscarf,
gold sunglasses reflecting the lights
of lampposts which are heavy –
headed swans with the sun
in their mouth.

he rocks with laughter.
his right hand holds the phone.
his left spins the chair in circles
like a football in the end zone,
a b-boy pirouetting, the balance
of a Globetrotter, a strained voice
recorded, revolving on a peanut.

KURT ELLING AT THE GREEN MILL

the bassist plucks slowly into the movement,
the drummer drops silver bristles over cymbals
like tears drizzling on a windshield,
the piano player fingers bones, smashes notes

    and swing
    and Kurt Elling
    jumps- the band breaks
    his voice, a trumpet between notes

      when i loved you...

he spitspatters beyond sense
sound like prayer, like this is prayer
    and Kurt Elling is the white guy praying in Black tongues
    and maybe he borrowed from all traditions and world cultures
    and maybe he speaks in all things Black and all things African
    and maybe scatting syllables between discordant notes is how he speaks to G-d
    and maybe this beauty was not intended for his tongue

tonight he speaks the gospel in B-flat
he blows the languages of all utterance into fire

and the crowd is burning and banging
and shouting at the stage. lost church goers
and the local postal workers are here
among the taxi drivers and ad execs
college girls and Wrigley Field beer vendors

all love the same tonight

this is the Chicago i found alone
in the cold hours of El train nights
searching for Algren in a city
with a memory as good as the barkeep
history eating at her liver

this is the Chicago for all gathered here
in wool hats, scarves, and goodwill jackets
with only enough pocket change for a well whiskey
wishing to forget tomorrow
and time
and bills

this is Kurt's Chicago
tonight. his gift to the city
his valentine every wednesday
in february, his love supreme pouring
lightly over the bandstand.

MARCHING MUSIC BEFORE BOMBS DROP ON IRAQ

a cellist yesterday
danced with curved body of wood
head on the shoulder of her lover
left hand tickling his tiny neck hairs
the right sawing spine strings with a silk bow.

monday
Mississippi Delta Blues amplified the honky
tonk walk man in a baby blue suit, Black button
down flared at the collar, white Stetson hat, sky blue
gators worn in from stompin on the devil.

tuesday
Woody Guthrie's ghost strummed the invisible
veins of labor movements strung through jackets
of 9to5ers who dimly recall history classes and stories
their grandparents sung of Depression.

wednesday
a budgetless school marching band on tour.
boys beat buckets upside down, hail storms
on tin roofs, a thousand hands karate chopping
the mayor's back at a press conference.

a skinny caramel boy, a lightening bolt
shaved into his head, throws the drum stick
in the air like a cheerleader he sends to space,
she returns to his hand as if on a string.

today
a man squeezes sighs out the lungs of an accordion.
a Steinbeck character, maybe Hungarian, a widowed
retired toothbrush salesman, recalls old world music
and its refugees, fleeing genocide sixty years ago

in the rush hour dawn of impending war.

LINES TO ELLIS ISLAND

we stand in line serenaded
by steel drums and accordions,
bodies wrap around Castle Clinton
in Battery Park. push cart vendors
hawk water, ice cream, photographs
of everything New York: Lennon, the Statue,
the Towers, erect and crumbling,
fake street signs, your name in calligraphy.

we are tourists, cameras and fanny packs,
cell phones and plastic bagged snacks.

i came looking for my Zadie's name,
George Marcus Coval
on a wall, in a ledger, a book.
it has been changed, anglicized, chopped
and mispronounced by so many bureaucrats,
i will be unable to locate it.

he came from the east on the Red Star line,
i return from the west on a ferry with families.

this is the difference.
for Jews america has been shelter,
safe house and hopeful.

for Black folks,
america might be kidnapper and oppressor
rapist and opposite of all our ideals
memorized in civics class

which doesn't make anyone wrong
for believing in the country's promise
for the too few, it must be worthy of the great praise
and parades. the people are not hosting riots.

but if we viewed our country's narratives outside
the pens of our historians and heard the dreams
desecrations and death marches this country drowns
in its atlantic belly, would we smile in the nostalgia
of this island,

if you are Black in america
where do you go to trace your past
which line do stand in to see your grandfathers' name?

REMAINS. JANE ADDAMS TOWN

Giants look in mirrors and see / almost nothing at all

– GWENDOLYN BROOKS

Jane Addams is dead
like Fred Hampton
who Chicago shot
sleeping in bed
next to his pregnant wife.

for she is ghost,
haunting the utopian.
the city and house,
built by her faith,
encompassed in c.r.e.a.m.
(cash rules everything
around me). ask uic
depaul
uofc
area 21 planners who dictate
and red line and run
over Pilsen, pave over
Maxwell St, who forget
what we look like
when we work with our hands,
when we hunger in tenements,
when we labor in unsafe conditions.

and who bought all the land after 1968
and who benefits from university village
and who wants Latin Kings locked in privatized cages
though they are sixteen year old boys who got left behind
in CPS (the Chicago prison system), and the renaissance

in 2010 will be repealing brown v. board and the schools
will again look like the city and there will be no crossings:
no Devon Ave., no Rogers Park, no Little Village/Lawndale taqueria,
no Hull House mash up collage where 2000 immigrants a week
play music, sip coffee, watch theater, read books, organize labor
and their lives, together in the kitchen close enough to smell
each other's funk and taste each other's foreign sauces,

there will be no one left if the planners remain undeterred.
if the giants sleep undisturbed.

this is conjecture.

if Jane Addams were a Black man
she'd be dead by white hands, at least
bound and gagged like the boss
did Bobby Seale.

you can't go into white folks homes
and get them cleanin up the place
unless they pay you for domestic work
or invite you in for finger foods.

Jane Addams' birthright wrote her among the wealthy.
her and Ellen Gates Starr and Florence Kelly and a bunch
of their homegirls; white women who flipped, deemed crazy
and prescribed bed rest, who moved into each other, out
side of marriage and single family homes, who questioned the nature
of domesticity. the home maker is maker of culture

and the culture is broad like the people are broad
shouldered, hulling hours in jobs that should be valued like the jobs of bosses
and the fate of bosses and the people are the same cuz we live
in the same house, where we hull and haul our bodies into public space
where all bodies should be clothed and fed and coddled and caressed freely
by the hands of doctors and cooks, lovers and communists. american these hands,
immigrant and chained, dirty and clean finger nailed, raw and stubborn. the home and public
space blurred or extended like the good and goods a citizen should be offered.

whose america are we living in anyway
who has the courage to say what could be.

who constructs the Chicago we call sweet
who tastes the candy, who is paying the dentist
who lines pocketbooks green
who blue lights corners of brown neighborhoods
who oversees west side stoops where children double dutch
who sends fabled blue collars over seas, who pioneers
who has déjà vu, who sees colonial too, like double dutch
who is from the place they are from
who knows what their neighbors want for christmas
who knows if their if neighbors celebrate christmas
who is family, who counts nepotism and legacy
who is confined to the grave and gravity
who is brave, who has bravado, who aches for zion
who has been told no and never
who wakes before the sun / for their sons
who lives though death is certain

Algren said
since it's a ninth inning town...
it remains Jane Addams' town
cuz the ballgame is never over.

and we need heroes
who stand up to giants

who carry a big bat to home plate
though the pitcher is throwing money
balls and the umps are in on the fix.

Chicago remains Jane Addams town
cuz Bill Ayers and Bernadine Dohrn
dream here and Haki Madhubuti builds
institutions and Lavie Raven teaches
in a high school mothers made
by refusing to eat until the children
of Little Village had the same quality
education gold coast children deserve.

it remains Jane Addams town
cuz Marc Smith is at the Green Mill
and Nikki Mitchell's at the Velvet Lounge
and there are men and women who can't go
cuz they work the third shift and their lovers
will miss them until morning when they will
pass like elevated trains close enough to touch
but never at the same station cuz there is work
to be done and Studs Terkel refuses to quit
and my father is in a basement trying
and the Cubs put on uniforms every season
and Rami Nashashibi is the Muslim Martin King
and Beth Richie wants the world to stop beating
Black women and their daughters. start freedom.

Sun Ra, Ana Castillo, Ang 13, Ken Vandemark,
Koko Talyor, Sam Cooke, Rick Kogan writes here,
Stuart Dybek, Patricia Smith, Cap D, Lupe Fiasco,
and names never spoken, faces covered in knit wool
tucked beneath the Kennedy, faces forlorn and worn
wandering Michigan Avenue, Lavel blind between
red and blue lines at Jackson, Oba Maja passing out
poems at the six corners of Damen and North Ave.,

David schizophrenic in front of the Wicker Park
post office holding out cups asking for change

who is asking for change

it remains Jane Addams town
cuz of the people
working for change
and the people
are working for change
and the people never really change
but stay working, toiling in the death
of industry, though the light dims
the people who work for change
know tomorrow is
ahead of them.

AFTER DAWN IN DANA PARK

there is an old Italian man
who picks glass and plastic bottles
like fruit he is gathering for a pie
from the short evergreen shrubs
rounded along the outside of the park
like a mote, a wreath, a piece of string –
memory wrapped around his finger.

his grey derby droops over the burned
wisps of a pipe. he is hunched
over the playground. eyes scatter
to collect the night's refuse
so children can float
between jungle gym bars
like squirrels or ferries,
tarzans or olympians.

save his breath, brisk
in the early cool of day,
he cleans without noise.
he is the un-anointed
saint of swings. his pay
comes from no city or state.
his only witness: earth –
worms who wake
just after rain.

PARTING THE RED, WHITE, AND BLUES
(A HIP-HOP POETICA)

RED

i once met the king of the red line train.
we rode from Howard down to 95th St.
pointed to pieces his crew wrecked, told stories
of racking, running from rent-a-cops, jumping from fire
escapes to L platforms. just before we went south
of Lawrence, said his daughter turned two tomorrow.
last night he painted her a birthday card on the outside
of 3rd and 4th floor apartment windows. we passed the building
turned around and Winnie the Pooh hovered over silver snakes
like a g-d in his raggedy, red sweater and a girl's name
emblazoned with crowns, flying high in Chi's dusk hour of return.

red is for the blood.

red streaks on warrior faces
tracking buffalo. warriors who grew
maize in the earth, wove mystic myths
warring nothing fight promises of slaughter
until peace broke bloody egg suns over dawn.
when the wind had a thousand names
and carried men the color of wave crests
on ocean shoulders crashing old world
cruise ships on new world shore lines
drumming red rum, red rum columbus hummed
mutant outbreaks in the red genitals of squaws,
erecting red light districts in West India,
erecting neon red casinos in Gary, Indiana,
southwest sand tribes serve red label
John Walker, where art thou
in the casino bin ho-chunk jackpot
of half-assed reparations?

red is for the blood

spilled into rivers and soil.
red is for the clay we would call Mexico,
for the giant ancestors in Californian forests,
for the sore nipples of new mothers feeding
their babies at three in the morning to stop
all the crying. red rings around tiny mouths
who have sucked themselves back to sleep.

red is for the big bubble gum machine
of pete rose Cincinnati, sky at dusk,
cardinals and robins, corvettes and mustangs,
beets and cabbage, apples and watermelon.
red is our diet of steaks rare, burgers pink, redhots
with ketchup the reagan administration passed as ghetto
vegetable acceptable. the elasticity of arteries swollen,
puffy colons, holed stomachs bursting with ulcers,
eating our selves to the bone.

red is for the necks of men who see red in their urine
who see red when red taped instructions are not followed
to the red cent of the red letter, who bull horn towards the red cape
underclass capitalism waves like matador in front of their red eyes.

red is for men who wrestle
the fear of falling into the red
basement nights over taxed with calculator
crunching budgets and bills, scribbling lead
into red line notebooks, rubbing forehead migraines
hoping the big red eraser will ease the pain,
wishing to hit a red button to clear memory.

red is for the blood

of Black children murdered
in Mississippi, Mama Mosley's fourteen year old
Chicago boy left like red meat Sinclair saw in The Jungle,
disfigured flesh, left to rest in an open casket.

red is for Detroit who sacrificed her only son
one afternoon in Harlem's Audubon ballroom.

red is for the summers and scares
that sent mccarthy into the closets,
sent Robeson and Richard Wright
running to red Russia,

red is for the brick roads of colonial Boston,
for Crispus Attucks gun down by red coats,
for visine needing motherfuckers who made it seem
he was the only Black man in beantown
and write history colorless.

for Sam Adams wild in the streets leading a crew
of working men onto a british ship to steep the sea
in deep red, browns while imperial troops dreamt
of morning cups and digestive biscuits.

our tea party is the red bricks thrown thru condos and corporate coffee
windows by Latino boys who are protecting their neighborhoods
from blanco bank agents encouraging pioneering. american patriots
stalked by red light shadows swirling in the alleys, for rest of their days
marked like red ink slashes on a calendar counting til christmas
when the next martyr will be born to die again.

when will we sit again
red like bull in the wisdom of the ancients
red like buddhist robes in mediation
red like the new trier point guard burning in the backyard
red like wobblies and communists on strike
red in the blood of your days, america
          perform your transfusions
your blood is tainted.

WHITE

widdle me this –
goldie locks just walks into some brown bears house
eats their porridge, sleeps in Mr. Bear's bed
and leaves before they return. she passes bone
thin through key hole tv dinners, heiress apparent
poster girl for our wet dreams, nightly in her nighty.
the bears eat off wooden trays, she devours white doves
poached in hollandaise, a lump of risotto over salt mines.
the moral of the story is she's never charged with breaking and entering,
putting her hands where they don't belong,

white is for the people.

my people. a blank page
of historylessness, sun dial compass's stuck
on colonial channels. zombies asleep thru time
travel, in boats of gold and beds of down
our fantasies appear when we wake.
the world over   ours.

white is for the people.

white only columbus CEOs smoking private jet streams.
white presidents in white houses with white walls
white washed on memorial day. pearl gates
around greek columned communities. the american dream
is white flight thru cotton skies.

white is for the people
who dine, engineer white caviar, skim
mozzarella, shuck oysters, clams, mussels, shrimp

on silver trays. everything served in cream sauce
country club cloth napkins dabbed on pink lips.
john wayne eats blackberry pies with ronald reagan
at the counter drinking white russian
kaopectate malteds to wash it all down.

white is for the people

american as apple pesticide, chopped cherry trees,
sheets strung soaking sun waiting to robe night
clansmen, crosses burning on lawns of new comers,
american as *enin meani minee moe*, picnics,
corked bats and brass knuckles,
viaducts and property values.

white is for the people.

the good guy, american hero.
david duke congressional campaigns,
italian-american genocide day parades,
thanksgiving plymouth rock CIA stock piles.
white is american as nativity lambs and puppet governments,
pawn brokers shuffling hot bodied oddities in the trunk of memory.
american as blue blood anglo-phile incest chlorine gene pools,
white as Sally Hemmings children, white as israel's government
wasp swarms and perpetual stingers. white is the color of oil
company presidents who send non-white kids to war. white is american
as forged epistemologies and counterfeit eponyms, historic hoaxes,
fraudulent metaphysics, cartesian clones, i think therefore i am white.
post-modernity is an ancient cover-up for french philosophers to bite indigenous practice,
re-package collage as pastiche, make the language inaccessible, foreign to its innovators.

Picasso painted African forms. where are Robert Johnson's royalties. mein kampf
eminem's melt in the mouths of millions and Grandmaster Caz can't get a record deal.

white is for the people.
my people who can't dance
cuz we're off-beat
w/ the universe
and we lie
and hide and lie
and steal what's not ours and we kill
in freedom's name
we rape and lie and cloak our secrets in blood
mask our rapacious practices in the myths of explorers.

we have everything

to lose.
it is our game.
we are scared to stop   winning

O John Brown!
arm the insurgents,
kill us with our own fingers,
stick self-evidence down our throats,
shoot and kill,
liberate us from the world of our faking,
great Buddha shot-gun karma!
blow our heads off,
slap the shit out of us,
chase us out our gates in the middle of night
banging our secrets together until they spark
a white hot, white light
that burns us
all.

BLUES

there is no better image
for america than Robert Johnson
at the crossroads staring down the christian
predicament of good and evil, the cross
of duality, the choice to move forward
or not, to brave this land that is not
our own. stolen, this blues.
sky
rain
rivers
oceans
blue.
3/4s
our body
politic,
planet,
blue
come
down!
make
mud.
Black blue feet
wade hymnals,
follow blues north,
evaporate like ancestors
who push steam engines,
all our industry built
on blues.

Robert Johnson picked his guitar
with teeth and arrow heads

found diggin graves like Kool Herc
did vinyl. grave robin / hoods both men
breakin, diggin breaks like railroads
at lunch time and fault lines, the blues,
the people, all those needles Herc saved
and polished, ARTifacts in the end of industry,
dirty needles scattered thru playgrounds,
blues made by itchin the scratch.

its what made Renaissance
spread Harlem like some legs,
brought Mississippi to Chicago,
Alabama to Detroit, Jamaica to the Bronx,
ethnic neighborhoods to the suburbs and back
again, all this moving, this giant diaspora
wandering, made Langston weary
making america see what she could

                                        be.

(blue)

Satchmo stuck his tongue and cheek
and neck out at jim crow, singing and signifying
like he did, all that smiling-can't-do-nothing-but blues.

Chuck Berry stomped one foot on the pelvis of white teens
and the low-fi stiff suit 3 marketer imitations later
called it rock & roll, later elvis made it a house hold appliance
like tupper ware, common like the cold.

Miles was too cool
for all that boredom humdrum doldrum dumdum
Coltrane too cold to let ledger notes stay seated

in big band white only hotel orchestras.
Bird flew the coo-coo nest

took western philosophic imperial empiricism and flipped it
like an Art Blakey drum stick,
a Jazzy Jay record,
a cold note blown blue,
notes so blue and raw
the Japanese made sushi
handed back rolled drum loop
samples Grandmixer D.ST cut to communicate
with other planets and when he got there,
Sun Ra footprints on Mars,
George Clinton's crashed mothership,
wrecked vibratos, discordant altos,
the insistence of freedom.

Grandwizard Theodore found it
in his mother's bedroom, an erratic sonic fracture
rubbing ears raw, glass shards on asphalt, again
the music sounds like the conditions of the people

ask a ask a James Baldwin or Brown
what blues this county suffers
and you get the same answer:
look in the night sky, blue is Black
regardless what white folks do, blues is Black,
Black beautiful the blues,
a history lesson
america can't seem to remember, the song
we can't bear to listen
to. drives us crazy, all that blue
truth telling it do, of white folks
need to be messin,
always be messing with the blues
to make more blues. but crackers get the blues too,
once they put the whip down and listen
go broke and holy.

Woody Guthrie's father broke
in the dust bowl. he wrote
for the okies, not the ofays, told stories
of Appalachia's abandoned,
his guitar read *this machine kills fascists.*

       and who likes fascists?
they are boring and predictable and pure
the blues is pidgin and messy and mixed
mulatoo kike zydego, bluegrass gospel, mud bottom
a stream of ancestors tapping you on the shoulder
like *yeah motherfucker* those lips are mine, that big ass
nose staring back in a picture of my great grandfather,
old shit becoming new shit, shit shit, the blues is dirty
and ancient and ghosts show up in the bedroom
and dreams and point backward, tapping you on the shoulder
we need it again, that blue yearning for downess,
for eternal inclusion and connectedness, the egalitarian
democratic principal, the call *and* response, cuz you can't hide,
in symphony hall lights dimmed and distant, opera glass anonymity.

Prince pissed on the crowd, at the 1st concert i went to.
you can see the sweat and bump of bodies in a crowded basement,
in front of a dj, a horned magician.

prison slave chain work gangs, humped and broke rock
and earth to pave highways and demanded the verse
be chanted, the call was made to be met by a response,
an amen, a loud affirmation, can i kick it, yes
yes you can lord, yes yes y'all, it don't stop. the blues

is roots music
america necessitates its circumstance,
demands its people sing,

scream and strum from the valleys.

blue is the secular come holy,
come watershed, come sacred,
come devil and commodity,

which way we walkin, america

i am at the end
                        of the country,

all before me is Pacific,
its waters lap the shore
and return, crash and cap and leave
stone and shell. this is your story america,
the return and return and coming of blue.

UP.S.
(UTOPIAN POST-SCRIPT)

THE MEANING OF CHILDREN

Chicago/america, your children are born
to travel underground, and supposed to get high
brow bootleg mega-mixes on old Maxwell St.
sundays; white socks, watermelon and churros.
we are born to over stand and glide high thru tree lined streets,
born to inter-sect, cross-pollinate and miscegenate,
blur all fences and neighborhood lines ever
erected, we
                           concentrate
in attention delirium cuz there is a city –
country to beautify –
                           we are born
to make the hole holy, throw-up and fill in
the widening gap between those who have
and those who have to rent, born to master-
piece the backside of Picasso's cold blooded bird eyes,
born to scratch-bomb the hidden underbelly of CTA
buses and under overpasses cut holes holy in chained –
links where beds could be made and we are born to wreck
freight train mural names emblazoned in the eye's night
of I-94 where Metra tracks chug suburban sprawl,

                           we Chicago/america,
the children of reagan/Daley, know all
the heroes are broken like our fathers
but who said you had to be
perfect, let's start with honest:
everything we love is stolen,
every melody and word and brush stroke borrowed
or muscled or appropriated from what came before.

let's be honest about what came before:

DuSable should be a college
at the mouth of the river just east on the north bank
paid for by chase and jp morgan and all slave made
institutions, *bring on the reparations* Sekou Sundiata
echoes in the departed air where his mouth once moved.

let's be honest Chicago/america
you don't understand us
you are kinda boring and won't listen
when we want to play you
our record since 1973

but now that that record
that that record that that
record sells
cheeseburgers and hondas
and that that record sells
more than imported beatles

i'll say this
i dig Bach
but do you know who Jesse De La Pena is.
i read Eliot
but do you know MF Doom is Zev Luv X
or that his brother is dead.
i wanted to but was too broke to see Baryshnikov
but do you know Wakka is the illest
b-boy on the planet and lives in a basement
at Noble and Chicago where he cleans
the bodies and rooms of old people.

Chicago/america
we your children are born to inter-sect,

cross-pollinate and miscegenate
blur all neighborhood fences ever
erected, we

                             concentrate

in attention delirium
cuz there is a city –
country to beautify.

ACKNOWLEDGEMENTS

big up.s.: mark eleveld and ron maruszak, my publishers, for getting in the ring again. all my fam (peep the bio). roger bonair-agard, willie perdomo, julie parson-nesbitt, elise paschen, michael warr, lisa lee, angel nafis (bb) and malika's kitchen Chicago for reading early and late versions of these poems. dr. madhubuti for all your words and the trust/ belief to take me in. bill ayers. adam mansbach. roseann adams. the jane addams hull house museum for allowing a poet to poet. first wave. ace deuce. mid-west building. louder than a bomb. check the method. teachers, students, community workers, graff writers, beat makers, in-the-lab emcees, i've worked with, who i will, who have reached out, schooled me. ira for getting my back. jon for opening the studio. bandit productions, eric, jw, brandon — can't knock the hustle. tim lincoln who made the beats. brett neiman who makes eveything i make look better. kirstin, my favorite. idris goodwin, my favorite emcee.

props to the editors of the publications where versions of these poems first appeared:

CHICAGO TRIBUNE MAGAZINE: SUNRISE, WAKING UP, NELSON ALGREN SQUARE IS A TRIANGLE

I SPEAK OF THE CITY: LURED BENEATH YOUR GOLDEN CALLING LIGHTS

THE DRUNKEN BOAT: WHAT TONY TELLS ME AFTER A READING IN SOUTHERN ILLINOIS, WHAT IT'S LIKE TO DELIVER PIZZAS IN YOUR 50S

2ND AVE POETRY: PASSING GENERATIONS

CHICAGO PUBLIC RADIO: THE CORNER STORE, THE DTC CREW PAYS TRIBUTE TO DICE

REMAINS. JANE ADDAMS TOWN was commissioned by The Jane Addams Hull House Museum for the annual Jane Addams Day, December 10, 2007.

LATE TO YOU ON THE BLUE LINE, WET JULY, MESSING AROUND, and THE MEANING OF CHILDREN were commissioned by the Poetry Foundation for the *Rush Hour Concert Series*.

ABOUT THE AUTHOR

Kevin Coval lives in Chicago near his father Danny, brother Eric and sister-in-law, Elyse pregnant with soon-to-be-niece, his Aunt Joyce, cousins Cheryl and Sasha, cousins Adam and Julie, their daughter Alexia (Lou), cousins Jill and Amy, and blocks of other cousins too many to name, great aunts in Michigan City, Mama and Don in Florida/Boston, Stephen, Lily and Skylar on Riverside Dr., Chuck, Lovie, Brit and Kimmy near Mickey, his mother Susan, and A in Az and Southern Cali, Papa Sy, Zadie George and Bubbe Pearl on an Oak St. Beach in the afterworld, though he wishes everyone lived in Chicago.

Kevin has performed all over Chicago/america, in seven other countries on four continents, and four seasons of Russell Simmons' HBO Def Poetry Jam, for which he served as artistic consultant. His writing has appeared in *The Spoken Word Revolution* and *The Spoken Word Revolution Redux* (Sourcebooks Publishing), *Total Chaos* (Basic Civitas), *I Speak of the City: Poems of New York* (Columbia University Press), and can be heard regularly on National Public Radio in Chicago.

Co-founder of *Louder Than A Bomb: The Chicago Teen Poetry Festival*, the largest youth poetry festival in the world, Kevin is poet-in-residence at The Jane Addams Hull House Museum, and teaches at The School of the Art Institute and University of Illinois-Chicago. *Everyday People* is his second book of poems. *Slingshots (A Hip-Hop Poetica)*, his first, was nominated for Book-of-the-Year by the American Library Association.

FOR MORE INFORMATION AND FREE AUDIO DOWNLOADS, PLEASE VISIT: WWW.KEVINCOVAL.COM